THE AI REVOLUTION IN B2B MARKETING AND SALES

Disruptions of AI on Conventional B2B Markets

Stephan S. Sunn

Davidson Global Partners, LLC

Copyright © 2024 Stephan S. Sunn

©Copyright 2024 -2026 Stephan Sun All Rights Reserved

Disclaimer:

This book may not be reproduced or transmitted in any form without the written permission of the authors. Every effort has been made to make this guide as complete and accurate as possible. Although the authors have prepared this guide with the greatest of care, and have made every effort to ensure its accuracy, we assume no responsibility or liability for errors, inaccuracies, or omissions. Before you begin, check with the appropriate authorities to ensure compliance with all laws and regulations. Every effort has been made to make this report as complete and accurate as possible. However, there may be mistakes in typography or content. Also, this report contains information on online marketing and technology only up to the publishing date. Therefore, this report should be used as a guide – not as the ultimate source of Internet marketing information. The purpose of this report is to educate. The authors do not warrant that the information contained in this report is fully complete and shall not be responsible for any errors or omissions. The authors shall have neither liability nor responsibility to any person or entity concerning any loss or damage caused or alleged to be caused directly or indirectly by this report, nor do we make any claims or promises of our ability to generate income by using any of this information.

Davidsons Global Associates & Co. LLC, Davidson, NC 28036, USA; All Inquiries of copyrights, and cooperation go to: Stephan.sunn@aya.yale.edu

CONTENTS

Title Page
Copyright
Preface
Chapter 1: AI on B2B Marketing & Sales
Chapter 2: Understanding the AI-Empowered Buyers
Chapter 3: AI-Driven Marketing Strategies
Chapter 4: AI in B2B Sales Games
Chapter 5: Building Your AI Arsenal To Sell More
Chapter 6: Democratizing AI for All Size Companies
Chapter 7: Beyond B2B: The Ripple Effect of AI
Chapter 8: The Human Touch in the Age of Automation
Chapter 9: Ethical Considerations and Responsible Use
Chapter 10: Implementing AI Strategies inside
Chapter 11 Actions Now
Acknowledgement
About The Author
Books By This Author

PREFACE

The author and his partners contributing to this series of professional guidance and industry best practices possess over two decades of experience advising multinational corporations and C-suite executives. They are esteemed thought leaders within their respective fields and globally renowned throughout their extensive professional networks. Prior to the COVID-19 pandemic, when international travel was unencumbered, they would convene annually at a rotating global location. Their first reunion following that worldwide crisis was imbued with a profound sense of gratitude for having endured such a cataclysmic event.

Reuniting with one another brought joy to all of us. Even more so, the notion of how delicate and short life began to settle in. The idea of documenting our business experience and lessons, successes or failures, to help our colleagues and clients was formed in 2022 when we gathered in Jamaica. However, with the arrival of ChatGPT and similar trailblazing AI technologies in late 2022, this small proposal gains urgency because we fear within the next decade these revolutionary technologies could transform our lives and society forever, and resemble what COVID-19 has brought to us.

The subject matter of this book series are the business domains we have supported clients worldwide last two decades, with the priority in the last few years. We don't claim we are the researchers or professors in the technologies, but the practitioners who evaluate, choose, and apply state-of-the-art technologies to solve business problems. The technology breakthroughs are not what we pursued, the critical criterion is if the technology solved the business problems with business values. This is why "Case Studies", "Examples" or "Lessons" are weighted much higher than the rigorous analytics of the theories in these business guides.

This authoritative book provides a comprehensive playbook for leveraging artificial intelligence (AI) to drive measurable results in B2B marketing and sales strategies. With insights from real-world case studies spanning diverse industries and business sizes, it explores AI's transformative impact on understanding the AI-empowered buyer, delivering personalized omnichannel experiences, boosting sales productivity, and optimizing operations.

The book offers a strategic framework for successful AI implementation, covering data readiness, talent acquisition, governance, and ethical considerations. Globally applicable principles foster human-AI collaboration, enabling organizations worldwide to harness AI's potential ethically and profitably in the B2B domain.

CHAPTER 1: AI ON B2B MARKETING & SALES

The world of B2B marketing and sales is evolving, and AI is at the forefront. As someone who's worked in B2B for a decade, I've seen this firsthand. Things have shifted dramatically from the early days of marketing and selling. During my career, I've observed countless changes in how businesses communicate with prospects.

In the contemporary world of B2B, where events move quickly, rivalries are intense, and customer engagement is the only thing that matters, deploying artificial intelligence today is not a nice-to-have initiative, it's a must-have platform. The modern B2B buyer is more sophisticated, more in control of every purchase decision, and more digitally prescient than ever before. They yearn for personal attention and custom recommendations. They expect seamless, delightful service across phones, tablets, computers, smart devices, and anything yet to come. Success starts with a deep comprehension of what your customers want, and getting to that level of insight is impossible without AI.

However, even though B2B marketing and sales have a lot to gain from AI, many companies aren't fully embracing the technology yet. The barriers are numerous. Siloed and inconsistent data. Skill chasms and ethical questions. There's a lot to consider—and it's complicated. With all this complexity, many B2B practitioners aren't sure where to start and feel overwhelmed.

The book is aimed to share our and our clients' practices around AI and give readers an actionable playbook for implementing AI technologies for their B2B marketing and sales, strategies, and operations.

Over the coming chapters, we will explain the key concepts, tools, strategies, and best practices that could equip you and your organization to unlock the full power of AI to drive measurable results.

Let's begin by immersing ourselves in the world of the AI-driven B2B buyer. We'll equip you with real-life case studies and fact-based insights on how the buyer journey is being turbocharged by AI—and what you must do to stay on the cutting edge.

Next, we'll showcase the latest AI-fueled marketing techniques—from wrestling ROI out of the data onslaught to orchestrating hyper-relevant experiences your prospects can't resist. Think of us as your marketing GPS, steering you toward the strategies and technologies that will:

1. Deepen your understanding of changing buyer preferences—and their implications for your marketing programs
2. Build out the capabilities you need to compete in the Cognitive Era, including data-enriched CRM systems and B2B personalization engines that touch every stage of the funnel
3. Organize your MarTech stack to maximize AI's promise and your marketing team's productivity
4. Evolve your metrics so you can demonstrate high-speed ROI and customer lifetime value to your internal customers

However, we won't just talk about marketing. We'll also dive into the fascinating realm of AI-powered sales where intelligent lead scoring, savvy chatbots and AI-driven coaching are transforming how B2B sales teams work. We'll show you how to build a high-performance, AI-powered sales engine that can identify the most promising opportunities, interact with customers on a one-to-one basis, and close deals sooner than ever.

Naturally, introducing AI into your B2B company is not without its obstacles. This is why, in this book, we're going to devote a substantial chunk of it to exploring the main possibilities and best practices that will allow AI to be successfully embraced. From constructing that very important data foundation to sourcing that all-essential skilled AI team, to measuring success and making sure that the use of this wondrous technology remains responsible and ethical; we've got a full-blown blueprint that you can approach with certainty as you move through the AI landscape.

Additionally, in this book we'll provide a variety of examples of how AI is being used by businesses in every industry and of every size through case studies and real-world examples. Whether you're the manager of a large enterprise with endless resources for AI R&D or a hungry creator at a young startup looking to slingshot ahead of your larger competitors, we will show you what's possible and inspire your own AI envisioning process.

Therefore, for any seasoned B2B executive who wants to stay on the cutting edge, or an AI-powered marketing and sales rookie, this book is your must-have comrade. After reading the last page, you are taking away the knowledge, the tools, and the tactics in your pocket to modernize and amplify your B2B business with the intelligent machine.

CHAPTER 2: UNDERSTANDING THE AI-EMPOWERED BUYERS

The rise of artificial intelligence has not only transformed the way B2B companies operate but has also fundamentally altered the expectations and behaviors of B2B buyers. In this new era, customers are more informed, more demanding, and more technologically savvy than ever before. To succeed in this rapidly evolving landscape, it's essential to understand the key characteristics of the AI-empowered B2B buyer and adapt your marketing and sales strategies accordingly.

The Evolving B2B Buyer Journey: Gone are the days when B2B buyers relied solely on sales representatives for information and guidance. Today's buyers are empowered by a wealth of online resources, social media, and peer reviews, allowing them to conduct extensive research and form opinions long before engaging with a sales team. This shift has led to a more complex and non-linear buyer journey, characterized by multiple touchpoints and a heightened expectation for personalized, data-driven experiences.

Moreover, the rise of AI has given B2B buyers a taste for the kind of hyper-personalized, predictive experiences they enjoy as consumers. They now expect B2B vendors to anticipate their needs, provide tailored recommendations, and deliver seamless interactions across every channel. Meeting these expectations requires a deep understanding of customer data and the ability to leverage AI to deliver personalized experiences at scale.

Another critical aspect of the evolving B2B buyer journey is the rise of complex buying committees. In many organizations, purchasing decisions are no longer made by a single individual but by a group of stakeholders with diverse needs, priorities, and decision-making styles. Navigating these complex dynamics requires a nuanced approach that takes into account the unique perspectives and influences of each committee member.

The Power of AI for B2B Success: To thrive in this new era of B2B buying, companies must embrace the power of AI to unlock the full potential of their customer data. By leveraging AI-powered analytics, businesses can gain deep insights into customer behavior, preferences, and propensity to buy, enabling them to deliver the right message to the right person at the right time.

At its core, AI is all about making sense of vast amounts of data and using that knowledge to drive better decision-making. In the context of B2B marketing and sales, this means leveraging AI to create detailed customer segments, predict future needs and behaviors, and deliver hyper-personalized experiences that resonate with each individual buyer.

For example, AI-powered recommendation engines can analyze a buyer's past purchases, browsing behavior, and social media activity to identify patterns and preferences, and then use that information to serve up tailored product recommendations and content. Similarly, AI-driven chatbots can engage buyers in natural, conversational interactions, answering questions, providing guidance, and even facilitating transactions in real-time.

Global Considerations: As B2B companies increasingly operate in a global marketplace, it's important to consider the cultural nuances and regulatory landscapes that may impact the implementation of AI in different regions. For example, the General Data Protection Regulation (GDPR) in Europe sets strict guidelines for the collection, use, and storage of personal data, with hefty fines for non-compliance. B2B companies must ensure that their AI-powered marketing and sales initiatives are fully compliant with these regulations, while also being mindful of cultural differences in attitudes towards data privacy and technology adoption.

The rise of the AI-empowered B2B buyer represents both a challenge and an opportunity for businesses. By understanding the key characteristics of this new breed of customer and leveraging the power of AI to deliver personalized, data-driven experiences, B2B companies can differentiate themselves in a crowded marketplace and build lasting, profitable relationships with their customers. In the next chapter, we'll dive deeper into the specific AI-driven marketing strategies that can help you tame the data deluge and deliver the hyper-personalized experiences your buyers crave.

CHAPTER 3: AI-DRIVEN MARKETING STRATEGIES

In the age of the AI-empowered B2B buyer, data is the lifeblood of effective marketing. However, many organizations find themselves drowning in a sea of data, struggling to make sense of the vast amounts of information at their disposal. In this chapter, we'll explore how AI can help you tame the data deluge, gain deep insights into your customers, and deliver personalized experiences that drive engagement and revenue.

Taming the Data Deluge: One of the biggest challenges facing B2B marketers today is the sheer volume and complexity of customer data. From website interactions and social media activity to purchase history and customer service records, the amount of data available can be overwhelming. To make matters worse, this data is often siloed across different systems and departments, making it difficult to get a complete picture of the customer journey.

This is where AI comes in. By leveraging advanced data integration and cleansing techniques, AI can help you break down data silos and create a unified view of your customers. Machine learning algorithms can automatically identify and correct data quality issues, such as duplicate records or inconsistent formatting, ensuring that your customer data is accurate, reliable, and ready for analysis.

AI-powered Customer Segmentation: Once you have a clean, comprehensive dataset, the next step is to use AI to gain deep insights into your customers. One of the most powerful applications of AI in B2B marketing is customer segmentation. By analyzing vast amounts of customer data, AI algorithms can identify patterns and commonalities that may not be immediately apparent to human analysts. This allows you to create highly targeted customer segments based on a wide range of attributes, from demographic and firmographic data to behavioral and psychographic insights.

For example, an AI-powered segmentation tool might identify a group of customers who have recently viewed a particular product page on your website, downloaded a specific piece of content, and engaged with your brand on social media. By understanding the unique characteristics and needs of this segment, you can create personalized marketing campaigns that speak directly to their interests and pain points.

The Personalization Imperative: In today's hyper-competitive B2B landscape, personalization is no longer a nice-to-have – it's a must-have. B2B buyers expect vendors to understand their unique needs and preferences, and to deliver tailored experiences that resonate on a personal level. AI is the key to unlocking the power of personalization at scale.

One of the most exciting applications of AI in B2B marketing is dynamic content creation. By analyzing customer data and behavior, AI algorithms can automatically generate personalized content, such as email subject lines, product recommendations, and even entire web pages, that are tailored to the individual needs and preferences of each customer. This not only saves time and resources but also ensures that every interaction with your brand is highly relevant and engaging.

Another way AI is transforming B2B personalization is through the concept of "micro-moments." These are the brief, intent-driven moments when a customer turns to their device to learn something, do something, or buy something. By leveraging AI to analyze customer behavior in real-time, B2B marketers can identify these micro-moments and deliver highly targeted, contextually relevant experiences that drive engagement and conversion.

Predictive Marketing with a Purpose: Perhaps the most exciting application of AI in B2B marketing is predictive analytics. By analyzing historical data and patterns, AI algorithms can predict future customer behavior with a high degree of accuracy. This allows marketers to proactively engage customers with the right message at the right time, rather than reacting to past behavior.

For example, an AI-powered predictive model might identify a group of customers who are at risk of churning based on a variety of factors, such as a decrease in product usage or engagement with customer support. Armed with this insight, marketers can proactively reach out to these customers with personalized offers, incentives, or educational content designed to address their specific pain points and keep them engaged with the brand.

Real-world examples of predictive marketing in action abound. One B2B software company used AI to analyze customer data and identify the key factors that contributed to successful product adoption. By focusing its marketing and onboarding efforts on these key drivers, the company was able to increase product adoption by 25% and reduce churn by 15%.

The Power of AI in B2B Marketing: As the examples in this chapter illustrate, AI is a powerful tool for B2B marketers looking to gain a competitive edge in an increasingly crowded and complex marketplace. By leveraging AI to tame the data deluge, gain deep customer insights, and deliver personalized experiences at scale, B2B companies can build stronger, more profitable relationships with their customers.

Of course, implementing AI in your marketing organization is not without its challenges. In the coming chapters, we'll explore the key considerations and best practices for successful AI adoption, from building the right data foundation to measuring success and ensuring responsible and ethical use of the technology. But with the right strategy and execution, the potential rewards are vast – and the future of B2B marketing is undeniably AI-powered.

CHAPTER 4: AI IN B2B SALES GAMES

While AI is transforming the landscape of B2B marketing, its impact on sales is equally profound. From automating repetitive tasks to delivering personalized customer experiences, AI is empowering B2B sales teams to work smarter, faster, and more effectively than ever before. In this chapter, we'll explore the key applications of AI in B2B sales and how they're revolutionizing the way businesses engage with customers and close deals.

Automating the Mundane: One of the most immediate benefits of AI in B2B sales is its ability to automate repetitive, time-consuming tasks. According to a study by McKinsey, sales reps spend just 33% of their time actually selling, with the rest consumed by administrative tasks like data entry, lead prioritization, and reporting. AI can help sales teams reclaim this lost time by automating many of these tasks, freeing up reps to focus on high-value activities like building relationships and closing deals.

For example, AI-powered tools can automatically capture and log customer interactions, update CRM records, and even schedule follow-up tasks and reminders. This not only saves time but also ensures that important details and next steps don't fall through the cracks. By automating these mundane tasks, AI enables sales reps to be more productive, responsive and focused on delivering value to customers.

Intelligent Lead Scoring and Qualification: Another key application of AI in B2B sales is lead scoring and qualification. Not all leads are created equal, and it's essential for sales teams to prioritize their efforts based on the likelihood of a lead converting into a customer. However, manually assessing the quality and potential of each lead can be a daunting task, especially for businesses with large volumes of inbound inquiries.

AI-powered lead scoring tools can analyze vast amounts of data on past customer behavior, demographics, and engagement patterns to predict the likelihood of a lead change. By assigning each lead a score based on these factors, AI can help sales teams prioritize their outreach and focus on the most promising opportunities. This not only improves conversion rates but also helps sales reps avoid wasting time on leads that are unlikely to pan out.

In addition to lead scoring, AI can also help with lead qualification. By analyzing a lead's behavior and engagement across multiple channels, AI algorithms can determine whether a lead meets the criteria for a qualified prospect and is ready for sales outreach. This can help sales teams avoid reaching out to leads that are still in the early stages of the buyer journey and focus instead on those that are further along and more likely to convert.

Smart Chatbots and the Power of Conversation: One of the most exciting applications of AI in B2B sales is the rise of smart chatbots. These AI-powered conversational agents can engage with prospects and customers in natural, human-like interactions, answering questions, providing information, and even guiding them through the sales process.

Chatbots are available 24/7, providing instant responses to customer inquiries and helping to qualify leads even outside of business hours. By asking relevant questions and gathering information about a prospect's needs and pain points, chatbots can help sales teams better understand their customers and tailor their outreach accordingly.

In addition to lead generation and qualification, chatbots can also play a key role in customer support and retention. By providing quick, personalized responses to customer inquiries and issues, chatbots can help to build trust and loyalty, reducing churn and increasing customer lifetime value.

AI-powered Sales Coaching: Sharpening Your Sales Edge: Finally, AI is also transforming the way B2B sales teams train and develop their skills. AI-powered sales coaching tools can analyze sales calls and interactions to identify areas for improvement and provide personalized feedback and guidance to reps.

For example, an AI tool might analyze a sales rep's call recordings and provide insights on their talk-to-listen ratio, the questions they're asking (or not asking), and the objections they're facing from prospects. Based on this analysis, the tool can provide personalized recommendations on how to improve their pitch, handle objections, and build stronger relationships with customers.

AI-powered sales coaching can also help to identify top-performing reps and the specific techniques and behaviors that contribute to their success. By analyzing the patterns and commonalities among top performers, AI can help sales leaders codify best practices and share them across the organization, raising the bar for performance and success.

The Future of AI in B2B Sales: As the examples in this chapter illustrate, AI is already transforming the world of B2B sales, and its impact is only set to grow in the coming years. As AI technologies continue to evolve and become more sophisticated, we can expect to see even more advanced applications emerge, from predictive forecasting and intelligent pricing optimization to fully autonomous sales agents.

Of course, as with any new technology, there are also challenges and considerations to keep in mind when implementing AI in your sales organization. In the coming chapters, we'll explore some of these key challenges and best practices for successful AI adoption, from building the right data foundation to ensuring seamless integration with existing sales processes and tools.

But one thing is clear: the future of B2B sales is AI-powered, and businesses that embrace this technology will be well-positioned to outpace their competitors and deliver unparalleled value to their customers. By leveraging AI to automate repetitive tasks, prioritize leads, deliver personalized experiences, and sharpen their sales skills, B2B sales teams can work smarter, faster, and more effectively than ever before – and stay ahead of the curve in an increasingly complex and competitive marketplace.

CHAPTER 5: BUILDING YOUR AI ARSENAL TO SELL MORE

As we've seen in the previous chapters, AI has the potential to revolutionize B2B marketing and sales, delivering unparalleled insights, efficiencies, and customer experiences. However, implementing AI is not a one-size-fits-all proposition. To truly harness the power of this technology, B2B businesses need a strategic framework for identifying the right opportunities, building the necessary capabilities, and measuring success over time.

In this chapter, we'll explore the key components of an effective AI strategy for B2B businesses, from identifying high-impact use cases to ensuring data readiness, building the right team, and measuring ROI. Whether you're just starting your AI journey or looking to optimize your existing efforts, this framework will provide a roadmap for success.

Identifying AI Opportunities: The first step in building an effective AI strategy is to identify the specific use cases and opportunities that are most relevant to your business. This requires a deep understanding of your marketing and sales goals, customer needs and pain points, and the current challenges and inefficiencies in your processes.

One effective approach is to conduct an AI opportunity assessment, which involves mapping out your customer journey and identifying the key touchpoints and interactions where AI could deliver the most value. For example, you might identify opportunities to use AI for lead generation and qualification, personalized content recommendations, or predictive sales forecasting.

Once you've identified a list of potential use cases, it's important to prioritize them based on their potential impact and feasibility. This involves assessing factors such as the availability and quality of data, the complexity of implementation, and the potential ROI. By focusing on the use cases that offer the greatest value and the lowest barriers to entry, you can quickly demonstrate the value of AI and build momentum for broader adoption.

Data Readiness: The Foundation for AI Success: One of the most critical components of an effective AI strategy is data readiness. As we've seen throughout this book, AI is only as good as the data that powers it. To realize the full potential of AI, B2B businesses need to ensure that their data is accurate, complete, and accessible.

This involves several key steps. First, businesses need to identify and integrate all relevant data sources, from CRM and marketing automation systems to social media and third-party data providers. This data needs to be cleaned, standardized, and integrated into a centralized repository that can be easily accessed by AI algorithms.

Next, businesses need to ensure that their data is properly governed and secured. This involves establishing clear policies and procedures for data access, usage, and privacy, as well as implementing the necessary technical controls to protect sensitive information.

Finally, businesses need to continually monitor and optimize their data quality over time. This involves regular data audits, as well as the use of AI-powered data cleansing and enrichment tools to identify and correct errors, inconsistencies, and gaps in the data.

Building the AI Team: Internal Expertise vs. External Partnerships: Another key consideration in building an AI strategy is the question of internal expertise vs. external partnerships. While some businesses may choose to build their own in-house AI teams, others may prefer to partner with external AI consultants or vendors to accelerate their efforts.

There are pros and cons to each approach. Building an internal AI team allows for greater control and customization, as well as the ability to develop deep domain expertise over time. However, it can also be resource-intensive and time-consuming, requiring significant investments in talent, technology, and infrastructure.

Partnering with external AI experts, on the other hand, can provide access to specialized skills and technologies, as well as best practices and lessons learned from other industries and use cases. However, it can also introduce challenges around data security, intellectual property, and alignment with business goals.

Ultimately, the right approach will depend on your business's specific needs, resources, and goals. Many businesses opt for a hybrid approach, building a core internal AI team while also leveraging external partnerships for specific use cases or capabilities.

Measuring AI Success: Tracking the Impact on Your Bottom Line: Finally, an effective AI strategy requires clear metrics and KPIs for measuring success over time. This involves defining the specific business outcomes and ROI that you expect to achieve through AI, as well as establishing a baseline and tracking progress over time.

Some common metrics for measuring AI success in B2B marketing and sales include:

- Conversion rates and lead quality
- Customer acquisition costs and lifetime value
- Sales cycle length and win rates
- Customer engagement and satisfaction scores
- Marketing and sales efficiency and productivity

By tracking these metrics over time and comparing them to your baseline, you can demonstrate the tangible impact of AI on your business and make data-driven decisions about where to invest further.

It's also important to celebrate and showcase AI successes internally, sharing case studies and best practices across the organization to build excitement and momentum for broader adoption.

The Future of AI in B2B: A Glimpse Ahead: As we look ahead to the future of AI in B2B, it's clear that this technology will continue to evolve and transform the way businesses engage with customers and drive growth. Some of the key trends and developments to watch include:

- The rise of explainable AI (XAI), which provides greater transparency and accountability into how AI algorithms make

- decisions and predictions.
- The increasing integration of AI with other emerging technologies, such as the Internet of Things (IoT), blockchain, and 5G networks.
- The growing importance of data privacy and security, as businesses navigate the complex legal and ethical implications of AI and strive to maintain customer trust.
- The continued democratization of AI, with the emergence of more accessible and affordable AI tools and platforms for businesses of all sizes.

By staying ahead of these trends and building a robust AI strategy, B2B businesses can position themselves for success in the years to come. Whether you're a large enterprise or a small startup, the opportunities for AI in B2B are vast and growing – and the time to start building your AI arsenal is now.

CHAPTER 6: DEMOCRATIZING AI FOR ALL SIZE COMPANIES

One of the most exciting aspects of the AI revolution is its potential to level the playing field for B2B businesses of all sizes. While AI may have once been seen as the exclusive domain of large enterprises with vast resources and data assets, today's AI tools and platforms are increasingly accessible and affordable for businesses of all sizes and industries.

In this chapter, we'll explore the opportunities and challenges of democratizing AI for B2B businesses, with a particular focus on the unique needs and considerations of large enterprises, small and medium-sized businesses (SMBs), and startups. We'll also share some inspiring case studies of businesses that have successfully leveraged AI to drive growth and innovation, no matter their size or budget.

AI for Large Enterprises: For large B2B enterprises, the opportunities for AI are vast and varied. With their extensive data assets, deep pockets, and global reach, these businesses are well-positioned to leverage AI for complex use cases and at a massive scale.

Some of the key AI applications for large enterprises:

- Predictive analytics for sales forecasting and revenue optimization
- Personalized marketing and customer experiences across multiple channels and touchpoints
- Intelligent automation of complex business processes, such as supply chain management and financial reporting
- AI-powered research and development for new product innovation and competitive differentiation

However, large enterprises also face unique challenges when it comes to AI adoption, such as:

- Managing and integrating complex data systems and silos across multiple departments and geographies
- Ensuring data privacy and security compliance in the face of evolving regulations and customer expectations
- Overcoming organizational resistance to change and building a culture of data-driven decision making
- Scaling AI initiatives across the enterprise while maintaining consistency and quality

To overcome these challenges, large enterprises need to take a strategic and holistic approach to AI adoption, with a focus on building the right data foundations, governance structures, and organizational capabilities to support AI at scale.

AI for SMBs and Startups: While large enterprises may have the resources and data assets to tackle complex AI initiatives, SMBs and startups can also benefit greatly from AI adoption. In fact, AI can be a powerful leveler for these businesses, allowing them to compete with larger rivals by leveraging data and automation to punch above their weight.

Some of the key AI opportunities for SMBs and startups include:

- Automating repetitive tasks and processes to free up time and resources for higher-value activities
- Personalizing marketing and customer experiences to build loyalty and differentiation in niche markets
- Leveraging predictive analytics to identify new market opportunities and optimize pricing and promotions
- Enhancing product and service offerings with AI-powered features and capabilities

However, SMBs and startups also face unique challenges when it comes to AI adoption, such as:

- Limited data assets and IT infrastructure to support AI initiatives
- Constrained budgets and resources for investing in AI talent and technologies
- Lack of in-house AI expertise and knowledge to identify and prioritize use cases
- Balancing AI adoption with other business priorities and demands on limited resources

To overcome these challenges, SMBs and startups need to be strategic and focused in their AI adoption, prioritizing use cases that offer the greatest impact and ROI for their specific business needs and goals. They may also need to look to external partners and platforms to access the necessary data, tools, and expertise to support their AI initiatives.

Case Studies in Action: Throughout this chapter, we'll showcase a range of inspiring case studies of B2B businesses that have successfully leveraged AI to drive growth and innovation, no matter their size or industry. From a small manufacturing firm that used AI to optimize its production processes and reduce waste to a global financial services company that leveraged AI to personalize its customer interactions and reduce churn, these examples will demonstrate the power and potential of AI for businesses of all sizes.

Special Insight: The "AI on a Shoestring" Strategy: For bootstrapped startups and SMBs with limited resources, the idea of investing in AI may seem daunting or even impossible. However, with the right strategy and approach, even the most resource-constrained businesses can leverage AI to drive growth and competitiveness.

In this special insight section, we'll share a practical roadmap for implementing an "AI on a Shoestring" strategy, including:

- Identifying high-impact, low-cost AI use cases that align with your business goals and customer needs
- Leveraging open-source AI tools and platforms to minimize upfront costs and risks
- Partnering with academic institutions or industry consortia to access data, expertise, and resources

- Focusing on quick wins and iterative improvements to demonstrate value and build momentum over time

By following this roadmap, even the most resource-constrained B2B businesses can begin to harness the power of AI and lay the foundation for future growth and success.

Conclusion: As the B2B landscape continues to evolve and become more competitive, the ability to leverage AI for growth and innovation will become increasingly essential for businesses of all sizes. Whether you're a large enterprise looking to optimize your global operations or a scrappy startup looking to disrupt your industry, AI offers a wealth of opportunities to drive efficiency, personalization, and competitiveness.

By understanding the unique opportunities and challenges of AI adoption for your business size and industry, and by developing a strategic and focused approach to AI implementation, you can begin to democratize AI and unlock its full potential for your organization. With the right tools, partners, and mindset, the power of AI is within reach for B2B businesses of all sizes – and the future is bright for those who embrace it.

CHAPTER 7: BEYOND B2B: THE RIPPLE EFFECT OF AI

While the primary focus of this book has been on the impact of AI on B2B marketing and sales, it's important to recognize that the transformative power of this technology extends far beyond these domains. AI is reshaping the entire business landscape, from supply chain management and financial reporting to human resources and customer service.

In this chapter, we'll explore some of the broader implications and applications of AI for B2B businesses, and how these trends are creating new opportunities and challenges for organizations of all sizes and industries.

The Evolving Customer Journey: A Holistic View: One of the key ways in which AI is transforming the B2B landscape is by enabling a more holistic and integrated view of the customer journey. With the help of AI-powered analytics and automation tools, businesses can now track and optimize every touchpoint and interaction with their customers, from initial awareness and consideration to purchase and post-sales support.

This holistic view of the customer journey is particularly important in the context of B2B marketing and sales, where the buying process is often complex and involves multiple stakeholders and decision-makers. By leveraging AI to analyze customer data across multiple channels and systems, businesses can gain a more complete and accurate picture of their customer's needs, preferences, and behaviors, and tailor their engagement strategies accordingly.

However, the benefits of a holistic customer view extend beyond just marketing and sales. By sharing customer insights and data across the organization, businesses can also optimize other key functions, such as product development, customer service, and account management. This can lead to more seamless and satisfying customer experiences, as well as more efficient and effective internal operations.

AI-powered Internal Operations: Another way in which AI is transforming the B2B landscape is by enabling more intelligent and automated internal operations. From supply chain optimization and financial forecasting to HR analytics and risk management, AI is helping businesses streamline and optimize their core functions in ways that were previously impossible.

For example, AI-powered supply chain management tools can help businesses predict demand, optimize inventory levels, and streamline logistics and transportation. This can lead to significant cost savings, as well as improved customer satisfaction and loyalty.

Similarly, AI-powered financial reporting and forecasting tools can help businesses make more accurate and timely decisions based on real-time data and predictive analytics. This can help to reduce risk, improve cash flow management, and drive more profitable growth.

And in the realm of human resources, AI-powered tools can help businesses to optimize talent acquisition, development, and retention strategies. By analyzing employee data and performance metrics, these tools can help to identify top performers, predict attrition risk, and recommend personalized training and development plans.

The Future of Work: Reskilling and Upskilling for the AI Age: Of course, the rise of AI in the B2B landscape also has significant implications for the future of work and the skills and capabilities that will be required to succeed in the years ahead. As AI automates more routine and repetitive tasks, businesses will need to rethink their talent strategies and invest in reskilling and upskilling their workforce to keep pace with the changing demands of the market.

This will require a significant shift in mindset and approach, as businesses move away from traditional, siloed functional roles and towards more agile, cross-functional teams that can collaborate and adapt to new challenges and opportunities as they arise. It will also require a greater emphasis on soft skills, such as creativity, critical thinking, and emotional intelligence, as well as technical skills in areas such as data science, machine learning, and AI development.

To support this transition, businesses will need to invest in comprehensive training and development programs that help employees build the skills and capabilities they need to thrive in an AI-driven world. This may include a mix of on-the-job learning, formal training and certification programs, and mentorship and coaching initiatives.

Conclusion: As the examples and trends outlined in this chapter demonstrate, the impact of AI on the B2B landscape is far-reaching and transformative. From enabling more holistic and integrated customer experiences to optimizing internal operations and reshaping the future of work, AI is creating new opportunities and challenges for businesses of all sizes and industries.

To succeed in this new landscape, B2B businesses will need to embrace a more agile, adaptive, and collaborative approach to innovation and growth. They will need to invest in the right tools, talent, and capabilities to harness the power of AI, while also staying attuned to the evolving needs and expectations of their customers and stakeholders.

By taking a proactive and strategic approach to AI adoption and integration, B2B businesses can position themselves for success in the years ahead, and help to shape a more intelligent, efficient, and customer-centric future for the entire business landscape.

CHAPTER 8: THE HUMAN TOUCH IN THE AGE OF AUTOMATION

Throughout this book, we've explored the many ways in which AI is transforming the B2B landscape, from enabling more personalized and efficient marketing and sales strategies to optimizing internal operations and reshaping the future of work. However, it's important to recognize that the rise of AI does not diminish the importance of human expertise and creativity in the B2B world. The most successful B2B businesses in the years ahead will be those that can effectively harness the power of human-machine collaboration, leveraging AI to augment and enhance human capabilities rather than replace them entirely.

The Irreplaceable Value of Human Expertise: One of the key reasons why human expertise remains so critical in the age of AI is that B2B marketing and sales is ultimately a relationship-driven business. While AI can help to automate and optimize many aspects of the customer journey, it cannot replace the deep industry knowledge, strategic thinking, and emotional intelligence that human experts bring to the table.

For example, when it comes to building and nurturing long-term customer relationships, human sales reps and account managers play an essential role in understanding and addressing the unique needs and challenges of each customer. They can pick up on subtle cues and nuances that AI algorithms might miss, and adapt their approach accordingly to build trust and rapport over time.

Similarly, when it comes to developing and executing strategic marketing campaigns, human creativity and intuition remain essential. While AI can help to identify patterns and insights in customer data, it takes human expertise to translate those insights into compelling messaging and creative assets that resonate with target audiences on an emotional level.

Building High-Performing AI-powered Teams: Given the ongoing importance of human expertise in the B2B world, the most successful businesses in the years ahead will be those that can build high-performing teams that effectively leverage both human and machine capabilities.

This will require a shift in the traditional roles and skill sets of B2B marketing and sales professionals, as well as a new approach to team structure and collaboration. For example, rather than separating marketing and sales functions, businesses may need to create cross-functional teams that bring together experts in data science, AI development, creative strategy, and customer relationship management to collaborate on end-to-end customer experiences.

To support this shift, businesses will need to invest in new tools and platforms that enable seamless collaboration and communication between humans and machines. This may include AI-powered project management and workflow tools, as well as data visualization and reporting dashboards that provide real-time insights and feedback loops.

Reskilling and Upskilling Your B2B Workforce: Of course, building high-performing AI-powered teams will also require significant investments in reskilling and upskilling the B2B workforce. As AI automates more routine and repetitive tasks, B2B professionals will need to develop new skills and capabilities to stay relevant and add value in the years ahead.

This may include a greater emphasis on data literacy and analytics skills, as well as expertise in areas such as machine learning and AI development. However, it will also require a focus on developing the soft skills and competencies that are essential for effective human-machine collaboration, such as emotional intelligence, adaptability, and creative problem-solving.

To support this reskilling and upskilling effort, businesses will need to invest in comprehensive training and development programs that help employees build the skills and capabilities they need to thrive in an AI-driven world. This may include a mix of on-the-job learning, formal training and certification programs, and mentorship and coaching initiatives.

Special Focus: Fostering a Culture of Innovation: Finally, to truly harness the power of human-machine collaboration in the B2B world, businesses will need to foster a culture of innovation and experimentation. This means creating an environment where employees feel empowered to take calculated risks, try new approaches, and learn from failures as well as successes.

To support this culture of innovation, businesses may need to rethink traditional hierarchies and decision-making processes, and create more agile and adaptive organizational structures that enable rapid experimentation and iteration. They may also need to invest in new tools and platforms that enable real-time feedback loops and data-driven decision making, as well as incentive structures that reward calculated risk-taking and continuous learning.

Conclusion: As the B2B landscape continues to evolve in the age of AI, it's clear that human expertise and creativity will remain essential to success. By fostering a culture of innovation and investing in the right tools, talent, and capabilities to support human-machine collaboration, B2B businesses can position themselves for growth and competitiveness in the years ahead.

This will require a significant shift in mindset and approach, as businesses move away from a siloed and transactional view of marketing and sales, and towards a more holistic and customer-centric approach that leverages the best of both human and machine capabilities. But for those that can make this shift successfully, the rewards are likely to be significant, as they unlock new sources of value and differentiation in an increasingly competitive and dynamic market.

CHAPTER 9: ETHICAL CONSIDERATIONS AND RESPONSIBLE USE

As we've seen throughout this book, the rise of AI in the B2B landscape presents enormous opportunities for growth, innovation, and competitive advantage. However, it also raises important ethical considerations and challenges that businesses must navigate carefully in order to ensure the responsible and sustainable use of this powerful technology.

In this chapter, we'll explore some of the key ethical issues and best practices surrounding AI in B2B, and provide a roadmap for businesses looking to develop and deploy AI solutions in a way that is transparent, accountable, and aligned with core values and principles.

Addressing AI Bias in B2B: One of the most significant ethical challenges surrounding AI in B2B is the risk of bias in AI algorithms and decision-making processes. Because AI systems are only as unbiased as the data they are trained on, there is a risk that these systems may perpetuate or even amplify existing biases and inequalities in the B2B world.

For example, if an AI-powered lead scoring system is trained on historical data that reflects past biases in the sales process (such as a preference for certain demographics or industries), it may continue to prioritize those same leads over others, even if they are not actually the most promising or valuable.

To mitigate the risk of bias in AI systems, B2B businesses need to take a proactive and intentional approach to data collection, preparation, and analysis. This may include conducting regular audits of AI algorithms and datasets to identify and correct for potential biases, as well as implementing diversity and inclusion best practices in the AI development process.

Transparency and Explainability: Another key ethical consideration in the use of AI in B2B is the need for transparency and explainability in AI decision-making processes. As AI systems become more complex and autonomous, it can be difficult for humans to understand how these systems arrive at their recommendations or decisions. This lack of transparency can create a sense of unease or mistrust among B2B customers and stakeholders, who may feel that important decisions are being made by "black box" algorithms that they cannot understand or influence.

To address this challenge, B2B businesses need to prioritize transparency and explainability in their AI initiatives. This may include developing clear and accessible documentation of AI algorithms and decision-making processes, as well as implementing tools and techniques for explaining AI recommendations in plain language.

It may also involve creating opportunities for human oversight and intervention in AI decision-making, particularly in high-stakes or sensitive contexts. By providing a clear line of sight into how AI systems operate and how their recommendations are generated, businesses can build trust and confidence among their customers and stakeholders.

The Future of AI Regulation: As the use of AI in B2B becomes more widespread and sophisticated, it is likely that we will see increasing regulatory scrutiny and oversight of these technologies. This may include new laws and guidelines around data privacy, algorithmic transparency, and AI ethics, as well as increased enforcement of existing regulations such as GDPR.

To stay ahead of this evolving regulatory landscape, B2B businesses need to take a proactive and collaborative approach to AI governance and compliance. This may involve regular risk assessments and audits of AI systems, as well as ongoing engagement with regulators, policymakers, and industry groups to shape the development of AI standards and best practices.

It may also require a willingness to adapt and evolve AI strategies and practices in response to changing regulatory requirements and customer expectations. By staying attuned to the broader societal and policy context surrounding AI, businesses can position themselves for long-term success and sustainability in the age of AI.

A Global Perspective on AI Ethics: Finally, it's important to recognize that the ethical considerations surrounding AI in B2B may vary significantly across different regions and cultures. What is considered acceptable or desirable in one market may be viewed very differently in another, based on local values, norms, and cultural attitudes towards technology and privacy.

To navigate this complex global landscape, B2B businesses need to take a nuanced and culturally sensitive approach to AI ethics and governance. This may involve developing localized AI strategies and practices that are tailored to the specific needs and expectations of different markets, as well as fostering ongoing dialogue and collaboration with local stakeholders and communities.

It may also require a willingness to adapt and evolve AI strategies and practices in response to changing cultural attitudes and expectations over time. By staying attuned to the broader societal and cultural context surrounding AI, businesses can build trust and credibility with customers and stakeholders around the world.

Conclusion: As the use of AI in B2B continues to accelerate and evolve, it is clear that ethical considerations and responsible practices will be essential to the long-term success and sustainability of these technologies. By prioritizing transparency, accountability, and cultural sensitivity in their AI initiatives, businesses can not only mitigate risks and challenges but also unlock new sources of value and differentiation in the market.

This will require a proactive and collaborative approach to AI governance and ethics, as well as a willingness to adapt and evolve strategies and practices in response to changing regulatory requirements, customer expectations, and cultural attitudes over time. But for those businesses that can navigate this complex landscape successfully, the rewards are likely to be significant, as they build trust, credibility, and competitive advantage in the age of AI.

By embracing the responsible and ethical use of AI in B2B, businesses can not only drive growth and innovation, but also contribute to a more inclusive, equitable, and sustainable future for all.

CHAPTER 10: IMPLEMENTING AI STRATEGIES INSIDE

Throughout this book, we've explored the vast potential of AI to transform B2B marketing and sales, from enabling hyper-personalized customer experiences to driving efficiency and productivity across the organization. However, successfully implementing AI in a B2B context is not a simple or straightforward process. It requires careful planning, strategic alignment, and a willingness to experiment and adapt over time.

In this final chapter, we'll provide a practical roadmap for B2B organizations looking to implement AI in their own operations. We'll cover key considerations such as assessing organizational readiness, developing an AI strategy, building the right team and infrastructure, and measuring and optimizing AI performance over time.

Assessing your organization's readiness for AI adoption: The first step in any successful AI implementation is to assess your organization's readiness and maturity for adopting this technology. This means taking a hard look at your current data infrastructure, talent capabilities, and business processes, and identifying any gaps or barriers that may need to be addressed.

Some key questions to consider include:

- Do we have the right data infrastructure and governance in place to support AI initiatives?
- Do we have the necessary talent and skills in-house to develop and deploy AI solutions, or will we need to hire or partner with external experts?
- Are our current business processes and workflows optimized for AI integration, or will we need to redesign them?
- Do we have the right culture and mindset in place to embrace AI and drive organizational change?

By conducting a thorough readiness assessment, organizations can identify areas where they may need to invest in additional resources, capabilities, or change management efforts before embarking on an AI implementation.

Developing an AI strategy aligned with your business goals and customer needs: Once you've assessed your organization's readiness for AI, the next step is to develop a clear and comprehensive AI strategy that is aligned with your overall business goals and customer needs. This means identifying specific use cases and applications where AI can drive the most value and impact and prioritizing those initiatives based on feasibility, cost, and potential return on investment.

Some key considerations to keep in mind when developing your AI strategy include:

- What are our key business objectives and challenges, and how can AI help us address them?
- Who are our target customers and what are their unique needs and preferences?
- What are the most promising AI use cases and applications for our business, based on our industry, market position, and competitive landscape?
- How will we measure the success and impact of our AI initiatives, and what are our key performance indicators (KPIs)?

By developing a clear and targeted AI strategy, organizations can ensure that their initiatives are focused, achievable, and aligned with the needs of the business and its customers.

Building a data-driven culture and investing in the necessary infrastructure and talent: Successful AI implementation requires more than just the right technology and tools - it also requires a fundamental shift in organizational culture and capabilities. To truly leverage the power of AI, B2B organizations need to foster a data-driven culture that values experimentation, iteration, and continuous learning.

This means investing in the right data infrastructure and governance processes to ensure that data is accurate, reliable, and accessible across the organization. It also means hiring and developing the right talent, including data scientists, machine learning engineers, and AI product managers who can help drive AI initiatives forward.

In addition to technical talent, organizations may also need to invest in change management and communication efforts to help employees understand and embrace AI as a tool for enhancing their work and driving business value. This may involve training and upskilling programs, as well as ongoing education and evangelism around the benefits and potential of AI.

Measuring the ROI of AI initiatives and continuously optimizing performance: As with any major business investment, it's critical to measure the ROI and impact of AI initiatives over time. This means establishing clear KPIs and metrics that are aligned with your overall business objectives, and regularly tracking and reporting on progress against those metrics.

Some common KPIs for measuring the success of AI initiatives in B2B organizations include:

- Increased revenue or sales performance
- Improved customer acquisition, retention, or lifetime value
- Enhanced operational efficiency or cost savings
- Faster time-to-market for new products or services
- Improved employee productivity or satisfaction

By regularly monitoring and optimizing AI performance against these KPIs, organizations can ensure that their initiatives are delivering tangible business value and ROI over time. This may involve adjusting algorithms, refining data inputs, or pivoting to new use cases or applications based on changing business needs or market conditions.

Summaries of Four Case studies of successful AI implementations in various B2B industries. These case studies will span a range of industries and use cases, from supply chain optimization to predictive maintenance to personalized customer engagement. The main purpose is to show how implementing AI right can improve companies' business bottom lines.

These cases illustrate the tangible impact and value that AI can deliver in a B2B context, and provide practical insights and lessons learned for organizations looking to incorporate AI closely.

1. A global manufacturing company that used AI to optimize its supply chain and reduce costs by 20%
2. A leading financial services firm that leveraged AI-powered chatbots to improve customer service and increase sales conversion rates by 30%
3. A healthcare technology provider that used AI to predict and prevent equipment failures, reducing downtime by 50%
4. A B2B software company that implemented AI-driven lead scoring and nurturing to increase qualified leads by 40% and accelerate sales cycles by 25%

Conclusions:

Implementing AI in a B2B organization is not a one-time event, but rather an ongoing journey of experimentation, iteration, and continuous improvement. By assessing readiness, developing a clear strategy, building the right capabilities, and measuring and optimizing performance over time, organizations can successfully harness the power of AI to drive business value and transformation.

However, it's important to remember that AI is not a silver bullet or a replacement for human expertise and judgment. Rather, it is a powerful tool that can augment and enhance human capabilities, enabling organizations to make better decisions, improve customer experiences, and drive growth and innovation.

As the B2B landscape continues to evolve and become more competitive, the organizations that are able to successfully leverage AI will be the ones that can adapt, innovate, and stay ahead of the curve. By embracing AI as a strategic imperative and investing in the right capabilities and culture, B2B organizations can position themselves for long-term success and leadership in the age of intelligent automation.

CHAPTER 11 ACTIONS NOW

Throughout this book, we have traveled a winding path, touching on the far-reaching implications of AI for B2B marketing and sales. From gauging the rising standards of AI-enhanced customers to basing personalized marketing strategies on data-driven insights to automating tedious sales chores to constructing whiz-bang AI-infused teams we have covered a vast expanse of subjects to illuminate the promise of AI for B2B.

The main points are:

1. The customer engagement landscape for B2B businesses is undergoing a revolutionary transformation at the hands of AI, with hyper-individualized consumer experiences, prognostic knowledge, and channel interactions conducted with ease.
2. To successfully implement AI, a company must take a strategic approach, including evaluating if the company is ready for AI, creating a vision for AI for the company, and creating a data-centered company culture.
3. AI is not able to replace the expertise of humans but rather strengthens them. In B2B marketing and sales, this power is used.
4. Creating a company that is enhanced by artificial intelligence will require a lot of investment in accurate talent, infrastructure, and relationships. It will also require a real dedication to continued schooling and testing.
5. Using AI in an ethical and responsible way is crucial to building trust with B2B customers and stakeholders, and for ensuring the long-term success of your business.

What is being said in the book is a call to action for B2B executives, he said. AI is no longer a futuristic concept, he added, but a present-day imperative. As the B2B landscape continues to morph and become more competitive at every turn, the companies that will prosper, he said, will be the ones that seize AI drivers to generate efficiencies, foster innovation, and create a customer-centric focus in the process.

However, reaching the path to AI success is never simple or straightforward. Rather, it takes the desire to challenge the status quo, to experiment and learn from failures, and to invest in the right capabilities and partnerships. Also, it calls for a deep dedication to the ethical and responsible use of AI; applying this technology in ways that benefit both your business and society as a whole.

Well, what do you do first? This book presents models, blueprints, and anecdotes to help structure your AI endeavor. But the critical starting point is to start at all. Begin by evaluating your organization's AI readiness, pinpointing your most promising use cases, and cultivating a culture of continuous experimentation and learning.

Let's remember the objective is not to simply put AI to work but rather to harness technology to propel our business and serve our customers. By keeping that northern light on the horizon and by being nimble and adaptable in the face of constant change we can put our B2B organizations in the very best position to thrive in the age of AI.

Looking to the future, AI in B2B will undoubtedly be defined by one thing: change. The pace of innovation will only continue to speed up, bringing completely new business models, technologies, and customer expectations that companies will need to meet to remain competitive.

But challenges also bring opportunities. The companies that can adapt and succeed in this new environment will be the ones that don't treat AI as a one-off project or initiative, but as an ongoing capability and core advantage, that can use data, automation, and human-machine collaboration to drive innovation, efficiency, and customer value.

Therefore, let us embrace this promising future with both hopefulness and accountability. Let us persist in broadening the potential of AI in B2B while also ensuring that the technology is utilized ethically and for beneficent purposes. And let us never neglect the human element—the ingenuity, compassion, and astute problem-solving that will always be the keys to triumph in the realm of B2B marketing and sales.

As we turn the last page of this book, I encourage you to keep the conversation—and the adventure—going. Share your stories, insights, and best practices with your peers and collaborators. Team up with your colleagues and allies across the AI ecosystem to create innovation and wealth. Keep studying and playing with AI's power to grow your B2B organization, and to change the lives of your customers.

AI has a glowing future ahead in the B2B world, and it's something we can action now. Let's be part of it, with courage, instrumentality, and a promise to all the good that's out there.

ACKNOWLEDGEMENT

In the creation of this seminal series, I have had the distinct privilege of drawing upon the invaluable experiences, insights, and expertise generously shared by a distinguished global network of esteemed partners and accomplished friends. Their direct and indirect contributions have been instrumental, and it is with profound gratitude that I acknowledge the indelible influence they have had on this work.

Kanth Krishnan: Managing Director at Accenture, has been a beacon of inspiration with his incisive insights and visionary leadership in technology services. His profound depth of knowledge and innovative approach have significantly enriched the content of this book.

As Managing Director at Newmark, Jeff Pappas has provided critical perspectives on the dynamic global real estate market landscape. His unparalleled expertise has contributed to a deeper understanding of the business environments explored herein.

Haitao Qi, Chairman of Devott Research and Advisory, has provided exceptionally enlightening perspectives on technology innovations and market trends, especially in the Asian context.

Formerly leading Outsourcing and Managed Services at PwC, Charles Aird's comprehensive knowledge and strategic foresight in outsourcing services have greatly contributed to my understanding of this critical business function.

Mike Beares: Founder and Board Chairman of Clutch.co, has been instrumental in shaping my views on business connectivity through his entrepreneurial spirit and dedication to bridging businesses with the optimal service providers.

It has been my great privilege to learn from and collaborate with these distinguished individuals and institutions operating at the leading edge of our industry. Any merits of this book stem directly from the exceptional global network of friends and partners upon whom I rely. Any faults or shortcomings are solely my own.

Last but not least, the unwavering understanding and support of my beloved wife, Biyu, has been an inspiration to this professional endeavor. The intensive writing workload harkened back to my doctoral dissertation at Yale a quarter-century ago. She remains the driving force behind my career growth and personal fulfillment.

ABOUT THE AUTHOR

Stephan S. Sunn

Stephan Sunn is the Executive Partner at Sanford Black Advisory, a preeminent global business and investment consultancy. In this capacity, he collaborates with industry leaders to advise companies worldwide on growth strategy, marketing/sales, innovation monetization, partnerships, and mergers & acquisitions. Over the past two decades, Mr. Sunn has consulted on sourcing provider selection for more than 30 international corporations and over 20 investment and M&A deals in the technology services, digital technologies, and global outsourcing sectors.

Mr. Sunn possesses particular expertise in empowering private enterprises to accelerate growth and enhance value creation through engagement with governments and technology parks. He holds a leadership position with Devott Co., China's largest private research firm focused on the IT, software, and technology services industries. Additionally, he serves as a Director at the China IT and Outsourcing Association. His clients span Fortune 500 companies, state-owned enterprises, technology parks, SMBs, and startups in both developed and emerging markets.

A graduate of the University of Science and Technology of China (USTC) with a Bachelor of Science degree, and Yale University with a Master of Science and Ph.D., Mr. Sunn frequently shares his insights and research as a speaker at global conferences and events. He is a prolific author and an accomplished presenter for his projects and clients around the world.

BOOKS BY THIS AUTHOR

Competing For The Growth

This book serves as a guidebook for city planners, economic development professionals, tech park builders, and public officials who aim to create thriving innovation communities that attract global trade and stimulate investments. It offers a structured path that begins with intangible factors like vision setting and partnership alignment and extends to pilots and full-blown magnet programs.

The book provides real-life instructions to help put these ideas into practice, including effective strategies for attracting rapidly growing businesses and talent, creating a setting that promotes innovation and entrepreneurship, fostering a competitive and appealing business climate, and building a globally recognized brand and reputation.

The author emphasizes that cities and tech parks must play to their strengths and assets to compete and win in the global arena. The race for relevance is on, and the window of opportunity to determine the outcome is closing. Cities and companies have what they need to succeed, and with the options, relationships, and guidance provided in this book, city managers and tech park authorities can make the decisions necessary to lead their communities to success in the world investment and trade arena.

Searching The New Profits

In the face of global market turbulence and domestic uncertainties, American small and medium-sized businesses (SMBs) and startups have significant growth opportunities in emerging markets. However, these markets also present unique challenges. This handbook provides a semi-analytical and semi-prescriptive approach to help American SMBs and entrepreneurs succeed in these rapidly expanding markets. Conversely, governments, technology parks, and corporations in emerging countries can utilize this book to learn how to collaborate with U.S. companies in their markets to serve their customers effectively.

The book covers essential themes such as researching and identifying matching markets, choosing the appropriate market entry mode, local marketing and sales tactics, effective risk management, establishing an active and reputable presence in the local market, ensuring full legal compliance, avoiding political involvement, talent search and retention, and balancing standardization and localization. The final chapter shares valuable lessons from decades of business practices, acknowledging that readers may have different perspectives on these topics. Expanding knowledge through diverse viewpoints is beneficial for U.S. SMB and startup leaders. Despite the challenges, penetrating foreign markets can be highly profitable, and U.S. enterprises have a reasonable chance of success by capitalizing on the vast potential of these rapidly growing territories.

Cracking The Winning Codes

This book serves as a comprehensive guide for international technology and outsourcing companies seeking to enter and succeed in the highly competitive U.S. market. It emphasizes the importance of adapting to the unique American business culture, which values innovation, diversity, relationships, customer-centricity, and results-oriented management. The guide highlights the need to navigate the complex U.S. regulatory landscape, including federal and state laws, as well as key legislations such as FCPA, SOX, and HIPAA.

The book covers essential topics such as understanding American business culture, complying with legal requirements, developing effective marketing strategies, employing successful sales techniques, addressing cultural differences, and managing risks associated with entering a new market. Additionally, it encourages the use of innovative tactics to differentiate from competitors and gain market share.

A special section titled "The Lessons" shares the author's personal experiences and insights, providing practical execution tips that focus on solution-oriented approaches, leveraging referrals and testimonials, managing communication costs, delivering higher quality than promised, and investing in proven local sales leaders.

By adhering to the core principles of understanding buyer preferences, continuous innovation, human capital development, risk management, customer-centricity, and resilient operations, global providers can successfully navigate and thrive in the lucrative U.S. market.

Win More Businesses

In the digital age, businesses must navigate the complex landscape of Marketing Technology (Martech) and Sales Technology (Salestech) to stay competitive and drive growth. "Win More Deals in Global Markets" provides a comprehensive guide for leveraging these technologies to enhance customer experiences, streamline processes, and boost revenue across international markets. The book explores the convergence of marketing, sales, and technology, emphasizing the importance of data-driven decision-making and cross-functional collaboration. It offers strategies for overcoming challenges in digital transformation, such as resistance to change and skills gaps, while also addressing the unique considerations of global expansion and localization. The authors predict future trends in Martech and Salestech, including the increasing role of AI, personalization, and emerging technologies like AR/VR and voice interfaces. Through real-world success stories from global brands like Coca-Cola, Sephora, and Airbnb, readers gain valuable insights into harnessing the power of these technologies for business success. This book serves as an essential resource for executives and professionals seeking to navigate the digital ecosystem and drive growth in the international marketplace.

Renovations Or Revolutions

The book "Renovation or Revolution? Impacts of Latest AI on BPO and Contact-centers Industries" provides an in-depth exploration of the transformative potential of artificial intelligence (AI) within the business process outsourcing (BPO) and contact center industries. It emphasizes the importance of early adoption, customization, and localization of AI solutions to gain a competitive edge in the global marketplace. The book highlights the evolving role of human agents, who will focus on complex problem-solving and relationship-building, while AI handles routine tasks. It also discusses the development of AI expertise within organizations and the ethical considerations surrounding AI implementation. The authors present a roadmap for incorporating AI, underlining the need for a clear vision, employee training, and continuous improvement. Looking ahead, the book envisions a future of collaborative human-AI partnerships, hyper-personalization, and proactive customer engagement. It stresses that embracing AI is crucial for BPO and contact center companies to achieve sustainable growth and remain competitive in the international arena. The book serves as a comprehensive guide for executives navigating the AI revolution in the global business services industry.

www.ingramcontent.com/pod-product-compliance
Lightning Source LLC
Chambersburg PA
CBHW072054230526
45479CB00010B/1058